How In The Morning

Write to us for our complete catalog.

The Spirit That Moves Us Press
Morty Sklar, Editor & Publisher
P.O. Box 1585-B
Iowa City IA 52244
(319) 338-0041

A 20% discount, plus free postage, may be gained by subscribing. The Spirit That Moves Us Press books are issued also as *The Spirit That Moves Us* magazine (ISSN 0364-4014), two issues per volume. Subscriptions are also available in clothbound as well as trade paperback editions.

The Outstanding Author Series:

Number 5—*How In The Morning: Poems 1962-1988*, by Chuck Miller
        4—*The Casting Of Bells*, by Jaroslav Seifert, 1984 Nobel Laureate in literature (poetry). We were the first to publish a collection of his in English in the U.S.A.—a year before he won the Nobel Prize.
        3—*The Farm In Calabria*, by David Ray
        2—*The Poem You Asked For*, by Marianne Wolfe
        1—o.p.

Bookstores may order direct or through Bookpeople, Baker & Taylor, Inland Book Co., Small Press Distribution, Bookslinger, and The Distributors.

Libraries may order direct or through Baker & Taylor, Blackwell North America, Small Press Distribution, Bookslinger, and others, and may place subscriptions direct or through Faxon, EBSCO, and others.

Chuck Miller's other books (listed on the Acknowledgements page) may be ordered from Chuck through us. Write for prices.

The Spirit That Moves Us is a member of the Coordinating Council of Literary Magazines. In 1985, Morty Sklar was awarded an Editor's Grant from CCLM, for excellence and vision.

HOW IN THE MORNING

MORNING

Poems 1962–1988

CHUCK MILLER

**With Ken McCullough's interview,
"Chuck Miller: A Poet Beneath Contempt."**

Number 5 of the Outstanding Author Series

**Number 4 was *The Casting Of Bells*,
by Jaroslav Seifert, who won the 1984 Nobel Prize
a year after its publication.**

The Spirit That Moves Us Press
Iowa City : 1988

Acknowledgements & Information

This is The Spirit That Moves Us Press' first single-author collection of poetry since its publication of *The Casting Of Bells*, by Jaroslav Seifert, who won the 1984 Nobel Prize a year later.

The cover was created by Kay Amert.

Some of these poems have appeared in the following books by Chuck Miller: *A Thousand Smiling Cretins* (Friends Press, 1966); *Hookah* (Friends Press in collaboration with Seamark Press, 1971); *Oxides* (Seamark, 1976); *Thin Wire Of Myself* (Friends, 1981); *Harvesters* (Coffee House Press, 1984); *from Oslo—A Journey* (Friends, 1988), and in various magazines, newspapers and anthologies.
The interview, "Chuck Miller: A Poet Beneath Contempt," first appeared in *The Greenfield Review*'s final issue, in 1987, in a slightly altered form.

Grateful acknowledgement is made of a grant in partial support of this collection, from the National Endowment for the Arts.

First U.S. Edition
Number 5 of the Outstanding Author Series
This book is issued also as Volume 9, No. 2 *The Spirit That Moves Us*.

1,400 trade paperbacks & 350 Smyth-sewn clothbounds (including an A-Z signed edition)—all printed on acid-free paper—were manufactured in the U.S.A. in October & November 1988.

The Spirit That Moves Us (ISSN 0364-4014) is indexed in *The American Humanities Index, Index of American Periodical Verse* and (some issues) *Granger's Index to Poetry* and from Roth Publishing: *American Poetry Index, Poetry Index Annual, and Annual Index to Poetry in Periodicals*.

Library of Congress Cataloging-in-Publication Data:

Miller, Chuck, 1939-
   How in the morning : poems 1962-1988 / by Chuck Miller ; with an interview by Ken McCullough. — 1st U.S. ed.
     p.   cm.
   (Outstanding author series ; no. 5)
   "Also issued as volume 9, no. 2 of the Spirit that moves us"—
   Bibliography: p.
   ISBN 0-930370-32-5 (alk. paper) : $12.75. ISBN 0-930370-33-3 (pbk. : alk. paper) : $7.00. ISBN 0-930370-34-1 (signed A-Z : alk. paper) : $25.00
   I. Title. II. Series
  PS3563.I37653H6 1988
  811'.54—dc19
                                         88-16062
                                              CIP

Contents

for Levy

"when i began this funny journey"

when i began this funny journey
it was the pumping thuds
the heartbeat of prose
that i loved
the clear sonorous hoofbeats of meaning
the people there laughing and weeping all over you
until you had them in your arms
and you fell down together
on the dancehall floor
amid the sawdust and sneering knees
the kicks and lost suppers

now i am beginning to love poems
eat them for breakfast
embrace them in my lonely bed
like lacey icing on cakes i eat them
an irish stew of the mutter sprach-ed world
venison of strangeness
they are my walking stick
my overcoat

the poets often don't say so much
leaving things out
turning into beautiful earthly ghosts
they are continually passionately whispering in my ear

and more than this
perhaps i prefer taking drugs,
and best of all is love

but i think it will be an old tipsy poet
in a great shabby overcoat
yellow decaying manuscripts trailing from his autumn pockets
who will
some spectral midnight

come stumbling   after me
and laying his palsied hand
upon my trembling arm,
say, ever so softly
poetry is a vast muttering
of what you always knew it would be about

mutter sprach: mother tongue

Requiem: A Surrealist Graveyard

there was Nadja's glove flickering somewhere
under the Madza bulb
which I think of now and then
an imaginary semi-transparent thing lost somehow
in what we could call a quantum of our love
a space-time geometry with its coordinate seam
unzipped onto the void;
does the void collect our mad love
surely the only kind which could exist
like a soft blue grave yard
upsidedown in a telescope eye
clasping us with the love of its ether arms
poor Mickelson-Morley trying to prove ether love with mirrors,
mirrors we can only disappear into with Huertibus
their love too fathomless for our mortal dimensions
but the ether wind spills down sometimes
wetting our seared black cheeks
and we realize it must be the kindly blue grave yard,
or is someone basting the earth in silence?
a great baked apple stewing in space
the gigantic spoon up-lifted
I hear silence running over the curve of the sky
but there is something I have lost
which we all wore then, remember comrades?
the good luck glove
I have lost the good luck glove
it kept me going in this rain of sad asteroids
I have lost the good luck glove
my hand like a socket in space
wanders already on that journey to another star

after watching "The Times of Harvey Milk"

you were moved watching him try
again and again for the board of supervisors,
and finally taking his place
among the other ethnic candidates,
how much affection he had,
it seemed to slop over in all directions
a voice of intelligence raised
and giving hope to that myriad of gays and minorities
the people warmed to him, senior citizens, Blacks, Asians
and he called to them to come out
from their closets, speak out
their true identity
the grave fear they faced that proposition no. 6 would win
and homosexuals across the state would lose their jobs
be beaten back and "Nazification" would take over
and the joy when it was defeated
they danced in the streets with a great outpouring

the enormous grief when he and Moscone were shot
the candlelit parade through the night streets
and the people marching silent
the great gulf of sadness wavering in the flames
the procession hovering, moving slowly forward
beyond fear

leaving the auditorium, you pass through the crowds
lined up for the second showing
and you see all the ones with the especially sensitive faces
you can tell in some way, some different sense of them
all the ones you will probably never know
the women beyond your reach, and the men also oriented
    askew to you
some of the women perhaps not so beautiful
who might have been judged worthless by the hetero sense
but most with that mark of inner suffering and knowledge

knowing the serious estrangement of
human beings who have constructed their own worlds
and burn with a special quiet radiance
waiting quietly with each other, men and women
in some fraternal cohesion
some of the men a trifle silly perhaps
but none with that look of casual brutality
Americans so often have
and most with some easy energy
and graceful kindness stirring now slightly in the dark
as they are about to enter
and see their hope rise and then be extinguished
and slowly rise again in a full measure of grief

you think of your lover who has gone over to them
found herself among them
who is now lost to you irretrievably
and all the lonely American towns they must have come from
harsh, drab, petty
each strange, shy, holding him/herself somewhat apart
probably suffering ostracism
knowing full well what it was
to be "stranger through our town"
the labor guy in the film saying
"and I probably would have thought the same way
if I hadn't known Harvey Milk, I mean that
when the cops went in and roughed up some gays in their bars
that it was alright to beat up a few queers"

the splits and shifts and chasms between us
all infernally trundling toward a lonely cul-de-sac
and I think these are the ones I should be with
but then cannot speak
and pass estranged and not estranged
under the dark trees

and think of the candles they carried
each one silent flame

something is winnowing us
winnowing us away, the chaff
from the wheat, but which
is the chaff
and which
is the wheat
our kernels are broken
we shift groping
in a sad wind

"coming west over brown plains"

coming west over brown plains
memories of displaced persons must be scattered
indians okies arkies all mushed together
thick bed of leaves under the primeval forest
gnarled and thinned out now
but still ancient stoical deep autumn brown
reminding me of ozark foothills clay pan of illinois
finally turn down the road we were looking for
grapes of wrath still stored here
ma joad standing withered and still
on a tumble-down porch at evening
floursack apron hanging lifeless at her front,
then a black man carrying a pelted animal
around back of his hunchedover tar-paper shack,
rouged western sky smearing into lake
backing the trees with pale fire
scruffy dogs patrol the environs with lackadaisical mistrust
old beaters crawled up and died in the mudcaked yard
some with their guts half torn out
firewood stacked agin the outer wall of a shotgun bungalow
that sits dead flat against the ground

i tell my danish friend the scene in which the police
come to the hooverville the joads are camped at
looking for troublemakers labor radicals
thinking they've spotted their man
they fire after him as he flees through the crowd
hitting a poor old woman in the chest, but it's nothing to them
as they take after him the preacher casey trips them
or belts them a good one to give him a chance to get away
when they get up stunned saying "who did that?"
casey stands there smiling calm possessed of his final grace
and says "I did," holds out his hands for the cuffs
i remembered the iron cuffs as they bit into my own arms
i tell her he submitted because he instinctively knew

he was going to get mixed up with those labor agitators reds
he had to find out   go to jail to meet the others
see what it was about
feel a lump in my throat remembering how they caught him
beat him to death
as he and tom joad ran through a shallow stream   trying to
    escape

later in the dark we see signs for mcalester salisaw
other stranger ones—weleetka?
think it must be belgian welsh cherokee?
then of a sudden turn
we pass through new modern industrial okie night
like some gleaming new city of machine functions catalyst
    crackings
lonely lit-up security guard pacings
same everywhere, in this exploited land

at a gas station in pulls a black with his young sons
driving a home rigged truck full of cut firewood
trembles and strains up to the pump,
stands high up on the front bumper
pouring water into the radiator
as the hood and metal scaffolding over cab cast him in shadow
we greet each other   he almost smiles
gives me a strange fleeting look flashing the whites of his eyes
a confirmation of something i'm not quite sure of

complicated joy

for stephen jonas

"in matters of joy we are all children
in sadness, gnarled philosophers
of despair"

for tom and martha, who upon the jounce
 in gather lights of refuge
  took an evening out of winter
    and taking me
pooled our warmth
    in my bed of high making
  even the dog wanted to join in
      our organs clasped each other in perfect naturalness
       the late night radio articulating
   all the complicated concatenations, warm skeins
    we threw over each other,
  the duke playing "tgtt," too good to title
   with a lady singer ah-ing it
    in long wordless expressions
some rich jazz pouring over us
              and now afterwards
        old lovers drift down
           out of some lazy floating heaven
           to say hello, and the bitter remembrance
         a mere bagatelle, in this stream that flows
                 in and out of time
      "wasn't that the Jazz Messengers?"
         brubeck taking "time out"
    we are strung,   a long jazz blow
     on the late night stations
        of the crystalline radio
            i sign off—
               thinking of them whom i have loved
               and those weird saxophones of fate.

Fatal Neighborhood

walking in dusk, I set myself adrift
down the old streets that I have seen change
even minutely . . .
the train yards with vague shuntings
low murmur of diesels
the stream strewn with garbage   running through the empty
   lot
but flowing clear and susurating musically
the people sleepy and withdrawn
hide themselves away in their half-lit houses
dogs bark far off
I come to the place where ours was runover
spilling her blood in the street,
then the closed-up Welfare Office
with a sign scrawled on it "Eating is a Right Not a Privilege"

how is it that I have lived here at different times
left twice expecting not to return
only to come back
for reasons that seemed to have
so little to do with me
yet it is mine this neighborhood
the darkened abandoned feed store
perfect and spectral in the dusk
everything is set to dreaming
in this August twilight
where my old house was
now nothing at all
they broke it down to splinters and carted it off
the church for lower middleclass Irish Catholics
always making me think of a church by Van Gogh
abandoned garages, oilsmeared weeds
all so ragged, desolate
peaceful in the gathering dark
darknesses that have fallen years ago

now fall again
memories come alive, flicker past suddenly
giving me an overwhelming sense of hope
and then loss
. . . the little valley of it
between two hills
like some Icelandic town
I have never seen but keep imagining
why this strange forlorn neighborhood
that against my will
I have grown so fond of
. . . surely like on's life
as faded and ridiculous
so these streets   which have so little to recommend them
become the dream-like streets of our life
the banks of my nightmaze rivers
down which we are always meandering
or hurrying with so much portent
and that at last seem so empty and autumnal
so homelike and sad
into which I settle   sitting on the dilapidated front stoop
there is no other

for Attila Jozsef

when the road was a thirst
down which I was drinking
and they warmed me bit by bit
even the heat of their bodies
was mine for the asking
and if it would not be love
they gave me a different kind of love
they gave me something to eat
they gave me, kindness by kindness
my life, which I held to
by a thread
just barely coming out of the fogs
just nakedly keeping on with it
because our spirits had been twisted out of shape
because we kept on coming
until she said stop or I will pass out

now from a bowl baked older than my dreams
I eat what is left
of the red Hungarian goulash of kindness
lately, it grows stale and dwindles
but the original
can never be completely diminished
—it's a good stew
to warm your skinny guts
in this time of hunger

of hunger so great
you almost forget how to take nourishment

for barbara

crawling out from under the hedge row
past the old rusted implement—harrow or?
through the stickery weeds and over the little creek
back up the dirt road that cuts through the corn
i wondered if my ancestors had done it the same
the men pulling up their trousers
the women smoothing down their dresses
better off for having done it among the elderberries
smelling the acrid dust of the gravel roads
then perhaps just mud
the straight roads intersecting a geometry of the imagination
that follows rise after rise on the prairie sea
listening off sharply into the distance
and maybe only hearing the faint rustle
of the wind in the corn
and the hum of the telephone wires
picking up a bit of dust by the roadside
stopping there to look, sifting
the september sun and the corn going brown
our intent wondering
what it might have been
the silent men getting into the buggies or model-t's
the women coming up behind
picking their way through the underbrush
what were they thinking?

that they'd done what seemed most natural
and whatever the outcome
they'd remember this day, or others like it
all the places they'd left their seed
their passionate forays or lackadaisical slippings
those that gave them what they needed for a moment
maybe they laughed as we did
realizing we'd returned to our origins without thinking twice
entered the earth again through the wigwam of smoke sleep

had our ashes hauled, as it's said
and strangely i thought of my father taking out the clunkers
from our old stove in the coal bucket
whatever else it meant slipping away from us
so we could smile our sad animal smiles
somewhat bereft of illusions
and think back on those who must have also done it thus
and become aunts and uncles and grandmas
spoke no more about it
except to muse occasionally in certain indian summer light
as though to themselves and secretly

you'd have to take these back roads for hundreds of miles
and into the night, cross the river into the dawn
for hundreds more and into the twilight
to find the remnants of their old farms
with broken pumps on cracked wells, newspaper for insulation
between the joists, the old pathetic implements gone to junk
in the crumbling sheds
a spavined shoe in an upstairs room
and then out to the cemetery to see what's become of them
the white-lime cementlike stones
now so frailly carved
just the names with the years and "his wife Marie"

as we cross the river the sky goes on illimitably
such that we might think one day there'll be room for us
in that big blue field
just as well join that vast hoedown
that's going on just beyond our reach
there grandpa will no longer be crotchety and severe
nor aunt bess ruined and crazy
all your brothers and sisters
who died as they tried to be born
will be there dancing a crazy irish jig

the music won't stop nor the cider keep coming

—if there is such a place
we'll lie down with each other again
in the grass and weeds
and do one of the few things
we know properly how to do

for Punch and Judy

the washerwoman has gone
the crazy one who drank too much
off to whirl her hurricanes through other hallways
lapses of memory, burnt a box of my manuscripts
thinking they were trash
her dog shat and pissed everywhere
but i liked him anyway
a purblind lunatic right from the start
yet perhaps she was my lover
and perhaps she was young and soft
and even had hope, and sometimes
a touch of the right kind of madness
she was not the washerwoman at all perhaps
or a pale washerwoman someone told me about
shrieking washerwoman!
one to wash my clothes in old age?
virgin washerwoman rinsing the filth of this world
irrational, this woodcut of memory

and now on spring mornings when we are a medieval village
    again
with its tradesmen, merchants, laborers
its hunchbacks, roustabouts, monks
its old women to market, its street cries
and mad urchins
my room is so empty without her strange clucking,
her bright dresses, and curious beads
her miscellaneous heaps of junk
"your life is a chaos" she'd say
or "you live in a dump"
i laugh at such old quibbling
but one evening i come home
and find my room full of ghosts
the washerwoman
who wasn't the washerwoman at all
has gone off

for Schnu

my dog woman
my cat woman
bear woman
times we were like prairie dogs playing in the grass
like wolf mates on the tundra
kitten woman
my otter woman
we might have lived imprisoned on the factory farm
pecked each other to death out of rage and frustration
as we teetered on the chicken-wire in our cubicles
perhaps for our wildness they caught us in the steel-jaw trap
and we had to gnaw off our legs to escape
maybe we are of the strange species Nietzche called "the sick
    animal"
my goat woman
brown bison woman
my laughing white-fish woman
now our spawning is swimming up different rivers
we are migrating toward different poles

in the preserves rhinos are poached and left to rot
only their horns are taken to be ground into aphrodisiacs
in the labs Copenhagen rats are bred to have genetic tumors
half again the size of their bodies
the electrodes are planted in the heads of monkeys
into the eyes of rabbits are delicately eyedropped toxic
    cosmetics
in the oceans porpoises are thinking strange thoughts
and must have already reached their conclusions

in the towns the dog fascists are rounding up suspects
to be vivisected and battered to death
in the most grotesque experiments
she watches over them
suffers for them

this hyena woman
with the tender hyena face

the elephants remember
as they are being killed for their tusks
somewhere a species is extinct and I am a part of them
in my dream a litter of mice was aborted
their pink naked bodies came hemorrhaging forth bloody and
    dying
I cried out for her to help
but she could not reach to me
these were our children

now in the evening the animals are silent
and grow sad with each other
the mammalian grief tints darker
my lynx woman
my coyote partner
with whom I have scavenged at the edge of cities

on the plains
the last wild horses are run down
to be shipped to the pet food factories
and put into cans
the earth's last mustangs
their eyes desperate in the sunset

my dog woman
my orphan girl
my feral companion

friendship

when you were both young
you shared those indissoluble moments so intensely
a wild beauty and hope breaking out in strange bursts,
many despairs

later in age the paths diverge
less frequency to your meetings
and the communions more rare
becoming the trapped gargoyles in the frozen chimneys
of the slow glacier of this life

there are silences between you
sometimes awkward
a banging about of the pots and pans
—the slowly cooking goose of which of you?
the "facts" are shrugged off—grotesque absurdities
or tossed up as comic tidbits
he says "I have lived a life ... more or less"
questioning and resigning with his hands
"so that if it should come ..."
and this rough estimate
of a rough life
so expendable for the others
so precious to him
... comes to seem in his gnarling
like some bristle-cone pine
dwarfed twisted out of shape
trunk along the ground
and when it shrieks in the wind
does it seem almost "inhuman"
or all too human for such idealizations
as we were wont to make of him,
now like some old man of the mountain

and sometimes in the silences

or in his buffoon-like mimicry
he seems almost not there
as though the pith of the being you knew so well
had vanished
everything given up

it strikes you then
that perhaps from a perspective you are blind to
such that it composes a dark wedge in your mind
your friend could be narrating
and you be the other, the observed

but then in a few rare attentions
a shadow passes in his eyes
a wing is signaled
that is enough
to keep the pact
so long ago sealed

Free Clinic

the basement of a church
one fan slowly circling from the ceiling as in an old-time drug
    store
a shabby clientel of exposed flesh swelters on this July night
yet we rest easy with each other
some maybe knocked-up, or with the clap
a urinary-vaginal clog-up, or needing birth control
a constant parade of people to the john
with their paper cups to get the clean-catch in its free fall
a kid acts up, his ma dupes neither him nor us
with her 'candied' "come here I have something to tell you"
when she grabs ahold of him she tells him alright
in a staccato of threatening whispers

"does your stream split?
do you dribble a little more?
when was the last time you were treated for venereal disease?"
old John asks then practices his blood pressures on me
I tell him then, I'm just now trying to get it down too,
this sphygmomanometer
I sit without a shirt, it fell in a puddle in the examining room
and meet some young guy
lank and intense
he tells me he takes medication for his anger
you can tell he's a little proud of it, this anger
"I get very military when I get mad"
this crack shot talks of M-30s, shooting the tops of bottles off
at a hundred yards, maybe going after Reagan
and how a girl got angry at him once
he felt sorry for her, knowing that she might provoke him
to some dangerous point
and what he might do (this last bit he recalls with juicy would-
    have-been anticipation)
he's latched on to some little hillbilly girl from South Caroline
bright as agate her eyes, you could spot her instantaneous

in a line-up of these bigger northern women
a little crooked somehow she is, ass bulges out
slightly bowed in the legs
and talks along with her man
a kind of vaguely threatening sweet hillbilly insistence
she's curious about me, looks me straight in the eye
as none of the others would
something subhuman they might judge her
yet she stands out   a more intense animal presence
some part of an old soul or body they haven't knocked out of
    her yet
she could only get a dollar something an hour in 1981 in South
    Caroline
after she graduated from high school,
so she came north where now she can vie for minimum wage
I overhear her tell her patient advocate that she's missed her
    last period
she'll begin her brood of young ground hogs, chippy monks
fighting hillbillies
maybe they won't take pills for their anger
but point it straight and make it stick

the medical student says cough, with his finger up my scrotum
feels up my ass with his gloved probe
he and John go over every possible angle of my trouble

in the end I'm waiting again without my shirt
remembering through the yellowing wallpaper years
most that I know end up here
on the edge of their rickety wood-slat chairs
waiting for children, prenatal care, fatherhood
abortion-referral, prognosis, pills
some cure or cure-all
grand central of the disenfranchised and malnourished

it strikes me then in a strange lapsed conclusion
that these others here are actually trying to give us aid
some kindness bestowed, care apportioned
patients' rights tacked up on the wall
no hot-shot medics here

the student pharmacist gives me my free prescription
and I go out into the sultry night
thinking of the vague anxiety in the women's faces
and imagine all the people lying up in their rooms
sweating, trying to fuck, oozing
drinking too much, getting high, listening to their children cry
wondering where their next whatever is coming from

The Guatemaltecans

these exiled revolutionaries
so free and natural
yet a few of them shy and reticent
what had they experienced I wondered
and whom left behind
whom no one would ever speak to again
perhaps in their pensive expressions
which would darken over
these were remembered...
but we talked of escritores
and poets, of who was muy bien
and excellente
and did we know of so and so
and they told us how at parties
someone would stand up—in the middle of the group
and recite poems
inflect with the voice and the body
the poetic rivers...
but here we agreed...people were almost illiterate
so I recited one by Stephen Crane
"but I like it because it is bitter
and because it is my heart"
they said perhaps this is the heart of all poets
and they treated us as equals
although I did not think I was their equal
then we began telling stories
and they made jokes on Pinochet and Fidel
about the soldiers chasing the revolutionaries
and the rebels taking sanctuary in a nunnery
hiding under the habits of the nuns
"and then because of your kindness I had to kiss your leg"
    and so forth
and of a parrot who died giving the finger to his enemies
then I told them some American stories
and oftentimes I had to apologize first

to excuse the racism or sexism of these jokes
yet even the women
those dark deep ones
laughed at the old sexual innuendoes
and even the Indian in them seemed to laugh
at the jokes on the Indians
as though we were all in one soup together
and I was a piece of carrot
and you a potato
but we swam in the same broth
I realized these were companeros from a beleaguered land
who were leading the way
and as they left for their Teatro performance
to portray the plundered history of their country
I thought, write your words well word-monger
for you've got to speak of this cutting edge
of these most vulnerable hearts out in front
who could smile or scowl or weep in a second
but who for an instant seemed dazzlingly balanced
as if in some laughing waterfall
catching the flecks of the sun

escritores: writers

"He had that tough scowl,"

He had that tough scowl,
a slightly narrow barrel chest,
his legs a little slight but hard, knotted
as though never having gotten over that childhood lack, thinness
—his face with black mustache, stiff-set, bleak
with a trace of a sneer—in a word: tough all the way around.
From one of the local factories, only a little out of place here,
he took a poke at a friend of mine once at mid-court
who deserved it, or at least the gesture,
for riding him unmercifully on defense, always in his face,
elbows, reaching in, slashing at him as he came across the key.
But because I gave him a lot of assists, some good passes,
when to the others he was something of a thug, and alien,
a cruncher, and because I was a good player
and point guard on most teams I played with,
he took a liking to me, cracked a smile,
said a word or two, a sentence;
and then just today as we came on the court
said he wanted to play with me
rather than against, as we lined up opposite each other.
Going at it he was fierce:
when you were tiring he came at you, hands clawing skillfully,
and you drew away, slightly, looking for a pass
which would set him leaning in the wrong direction
and out of the play.
When we had lost and were down waiting for the next game
they fouled him badly as he drove without hesitation
for the basket, again and again;
and I watched in slow motion his grim drives
as though at some line of scrimmage.
Then she came, sat waiting on the bench
as we went through winning a game or two
—slight, with baggy drawers, not much in front,
but a veteran, as you could see, with a rhythm to her
with that seeming casual quick low arc to her shot

that some players have.
To play with women, always made me curious
to test their responses, feel the comradeship or struggle with
    them
to watch their different moves, gestures, appraising;
somehow too they softened the game
—the men were less mean in their presence,
there was a sense of watching out for them,
and the others too were given leeway.
We played a couple of games against her team
which had my crusty friend at point,
and she played in terms of the team—some good shovel passes
as she came past and they would break—
take her arcless shots, some went in
screened me once,
and I felt the force of her body as we collided
—a bit short, sort of a rover around the court either way
with a faint sense of feistiness in her definite moves.
They beat us two games by a single point.
As the game broke up and new players came flooding onto the
    court
—always it seemed as the years went, faster and younger—
she came up to me and clasped my hand.
"Good game," she said, and we smiled at one another;
and I remembered when they'd been sorting shirts and skins
she had made as though to doff her top in joking gesture
—the warm electricity flowed through me,
the sweat and pulse of her hand;
and then as the three of us sat on the bench
he told us they'd been "tough games"
those two they had taken,
and smiled with a flush.
As he left I noticed the hard-muscled arms
and his skin, always a little dark,
a bit unhealthy, or so it seemed,

as from poor food or lack of sleep
—maybe he worked the graveyard:
the pockets of dark under his eyes
as though some factory black
or grey sadness;
but I had been lucky
to brush so close
and almost touch these two.

How In The Morning

why always in the morning?
because you must begin your life over again each morning
fumble for your shoes
the leather thongs stiff and cold
fumble with your fly
make sure your prick doesn't get caught in the zipper
by then the shadows are stealing up grey and clean
the sun a later gamble
that might make it through this hung over sky
then the long walk out from the private shack of our dreams
barely holding together
to the car which is slowly disintegrating
if you can get it going
drive toward the world
only just functioning on the grey edge of night
with its slouched coffee slurpers   its unconscious donut gobblers
its shoe factories stitching on soles
for the tender feet of our souls
its bellowing trucks, posts and positions
sinecures, backbreaking sweats
being fed the slimy exhausts
of the constant velvet farts of our metal skins
sewn onto us,
and it is all simple, grey, clear
if you don't think about it
there are those with their great life's works
and those who must do these very same great life's works
maybe Vallejo is riding with you this morning
looking for work the same as you
and he says "Understanding that he knows I love him,
that I hate him with affection
and to me he is in sum indifferent, I signal to him,
he comes, and I embrace him, moved,
So What! Moved ... Moved."
and I say to him "that was damn good Cesar,

should we try the employment office today
or the toilet paper factory   should we try
the donut factory once more to make that graveyard donut shift
or maybe the mental hospital
to see if they have an opening in the laundry
I used to do the laundry thing folded sheets
off the mangle
Cesar is saying "go for the pop bottles, fuck all this other stuff
these wood-bees, let's just collect pop bottles
that's the surest way"
and so the morning comes grey over the hills
you drop the washcloth on your cold feet
and fumble with the delicate
birds of morning
opening their cages

"i write for those unknown . . ."

i write for those unknown who were born unknown
who sat up in bed years later born again
and died unknown even to themselves
who could not know what i say
i write for verlaine still praying the pietas
in his cell in belgium
i write because i cannot sleep for having visions
for van gogh who splashes my wall with joy
and who painted absolute reality
i saw this and was unalterably changed
i write because i return to my bed at night like a convict to his
    cell
i write because i have given up all hope
and do not even know what i say
i write for no reason at all
because time is running out
and nothing ever changes
i write because there is a vast commune spread over the earth
and we are all touching hands in the mist
laughing gently and with compassion
i write because nothing comes back
and i have lost treasures of the wildest imaginings
i write because i am chewing the last rag of solitude
and still find a kind of delirious nourishment there
i write because when i opened my pipes
out came a pineapple made of pain
i write to have my 2 cents worth of erratic song
and be a part of the collective madness
i write because i am soon to sleep
and will rise tomorrow
to hawk my bones on the streets
just as you in your turn
will stumble half conscious
from your dwelling
we will bump clumsily into one another

step back squinteyed and suspicious
not recognizing nor understanding
go our blinded ways

"speak   if you can"

speak   if you can
for those never expected nor allowed to
whose words are Xed out as soon as they are uttered
whose song then modulates at a frequency
that can't be received by the official classes,
whose voices dropped from the roles
expunged from the annals
except that they were never there to begin with

so that if they exist as less than bit players
in a history which isn't theirs
it is to an empty theatre
they must present their stuttering orations
into which they must project their mute
but eloquent gestures

those who dream of being even a janitor
in the darkened theatre
to shake their mops and make the shadows dance

armed love

for susan

behind the bullet-proof glass of the visiting chamber
at some remove from intimacy
her hair astray, the woman turnkey had to wake her
sleep still turgid in her face
her sullen bitterness—some blackness running through her
distrusting then the whole fabric of life
and me, probably with good reason,
telling me her disheveled dreams
her children they had taken from her
a few years before
come to her in sleep and quietly ask
for certain things they need, a glass of milk
a hug perhaps
or a coloring book in which their double script had been
   recorded

the psychiatrists at the classification center
had sat in a group around her
and humiliated what shred of dignity she had left
calling her a cheap slut
with no sense of responsibility to society
she challenged them, fought back
she liked the other convicts there
who were kind to her
clueing her on what she had to face
her lawyer who had questioned her copping a plea
but he had never faced a stiff mandatory term
for being an accessory to a stick-up

she would laugh suddenly
as though it were forced out of her
flint striking spark
came out hard but clear
her parents had never approved of her
or wanted her—so much as given her a gesture of affection

although they were supposed "respectable pillars"
she had to almost trust me—to tell me that,
her thin body—unloved face—eyes almost scrutinizing
me separately from different distances
her futile future, "I can't imagine working"
and i knew what she meant (though we met changing shifts
at a private nursing gig)
some menial shit job with the bosses always running game
we talked on some telephonic arrangement
as if in a long distance nightmare of deliberate alienation
she being in the condemned dimension
into which no breath could pass
her case worker, who when she told of her childhood
dismissed what she had said with the quip
"well, we all have to get over that"
and went on rambling the bureaucratic ins and outs

sick of men who had beaten her
of society with its endless lies
sick of her own alcoholism, coke-head
her last lover had thrown out all her belongings in the trash
her clothes, mementos

i remembered other days
when her face seemed to bloom up
a spring light shown through
when she had a wit and told funny stories
about the old days of getting high
her clairvoyant experiences which no one believed
thinking her somewhat mad,
wearing her oversize prisoners coveralls—a luminous embittered
    child
—but lucid,
and laughing it down
as though in tender consideration of the strange absurdity of
    things

how most of all she loved to dance
i had never seen her
and could only imagine the lithe and light
of her slender foxing and flying
she talked of other years when she had some dreams
a lover "who was like my other half, do you know?
I thought he was the other half of myself that I had found,
now they say he's paranoid schiz and never talks"

in some years when it's over she plans to change her name
shed her father's, and her ex-husband's
and take on her great grandmother's whom she never knew
"they say she left her husband and kids on a farm
and went off with another man
I figure I'm like her"
the screw comes for her
"I have to go," she says now suddenly cold and blank
as though a time were finished
and certain walls cannot be transcended

outward, through the series of "decompression chambers"
feeling the deep reverberations of remote-controlled locks in
    your bones
as they clank you free
in a far echo of memory
i hear old convicts whisper of daughters gone astray
and sons doing time in other states
of the final lock-up

"paranoid dream police"

paranoid dream police
come softly in night
like a black cat's paw
silent on a windowsill
dreaming they float in
and slowly their jackolantern masks
leer the terrible teeth of the rubber smile
"we have come for you"

and i in the cabinet of dr. caligari
walking in the insane parks of the mind
sometimes thinking i am in paradise

from a great distance
specks on the horizon of a plain
the net floating toward me

in the entrails of a giant clock
swirling through springs and wheels
time enslaved in this madream of mechanism
will ever the larkbell to freedom breakpealing?
miraculous! the great cuckoo of absurdity
plunges agawk before me, and mocks its master
it has freed itself
yanked the strings from its heart
flies away through the trees cuckooing wildly
i follow making my own absurd love calls
i hear a band, a flute, the snares, a parade
thronging toward me they come
danton, tristan tzara, andy panda, donald duck
mary jane and sniffles, marat, kurt schwitters
tim west, the katzenjammer kids, all my friends and relatives
creatures from all dimensions
we are saved, reunited, innocence come back!
clowns on bicycles, angels making love

christmas on earth!
the clock explodes a carnival of fireworks
time flung its fiery wheels
historic springs into the infinite
oh god, we are in heaven

but no, the doors of eternity are closing
the light disappearing
i am in my room again, alone

and the paranoid dream police
come softly as a dark cat's paw
silent on a windowsill
as though not to disturb
the mourners at a funeral
and i in the cabinet of dr. caligari
walking in the insane park of the mind
sometimes dreaming i am in paradise

the voice from the radio
— this evening in the suburbs of Buenos Aires

when you were a child they sounded in their great wisdom
those all-knowing tones with the objectified voices
speaking in the code-like dots and dashes of emphasis and
    intonations
that you did not know—nor had any idea of the metamessages
you stood in awe of these casters broad
ah to be one of them, to be selected
to give the news
to sum up in your voice and gravity the events of the day
blocking history into its summarizable scenes
you saw them in your mind's eye sitting at their small tables
speaking into the microphone which came down from the
    ceiling
as though God or the sky powers had dropped an audio
to facilitate their serious and mellifluous voices
staring trance-like into the red "on the air" lights
from their glassed-in cubicles—
or then on television looking straight into our eyes
then glancing down to ground themselves in the script
nothing could be serious beyond these voices
nothing could exist beyond the focus
of their selection of the newsworthy
their tables broadened, adding "wings"
becoming the great broad table of intellectual consideration
capable of holding whatever material necessary
for their cogent lucubrations they essayed each day
or for confabbing with other specialists or sidekicks

you saw your classmates pretending to "give the news"
competing in junior contests, strictured in their first suits
hair plastered down
reading in their adolescent voices
as though they, now, ascending the serious stairway . . .
trying like some fly-caster

to end the particular broadcast
in the shortest number of seconds before the official
six and a half minutes of news was up ...

oh "history" that has been pumped into us all our lives
like embalming-type fluid into one of the voodoo undead
... of bits of news that are fat-soluble
and like yellowed newsprint lodge somewhere
in the forgotten warehouses of the soul
oh narcotic saddener and objectifier unto death
that does not need to be administered orally or by injection
but is taken voluntarily by the subject
so that history may speak in his ear
or so he hears

oh vision of Death himself reading the news

oh bought men and women
who learn that intelligence is filtered
through finer and finer meshes
strictured in closer   and closer   confines
until only the tiniest understated sympathy
for the junta's version is necessary
like some highly paid hoop star shaving points more and more
    subtley
and the smallest micron of approbation
for the "freedom fighter" guerillas,
until the selection of questions for the interviewed
earmarks the answers to be believed or discarded

now you almost feel a pity for them
like a chained dog told when to bark
the bought voice never able to speak some personal conviction
the emotions that must be hedged and hedged again
they must know sometimes that the innocent

are dying in their grammatical pauses
in their elisions whole sub-races are going under
in their versions justice is gagged and muffled
and yet,   they speak on
in those carefully modulated tones
which seem almost human, almost friendly, almost intelligent
as though they were singing to themselves
the song of the news, the serious and carefully monitored news
as though newsbrother were watching out for you
and when certain subfactions of alleged splinter-groups
are said to be liquidated
newsbrother will read your personal obituary perhaps
and the women now newly admitted, newssister
with their sophisticated and cold voices
they too of the frozen intelligence
of the numbed sensibility
perhaps in their beds at night they cannot sleep

in the evening when the dark comes
and we are returned to our isolated moorings
the magical and hearth-like dial of the radio warms us
and we listen . . . deep into the night
and for the news
listening between the lines
to catch a few of the silent Morse-like SOS of sinking human
     ships
they inadvertently let through
events which are almost interpreted
except for the omission of a few subtle details
which make all the difference
and into which we fill in the vague shapes
with educated guesses or intuitions
like the blind desperately struggling to conceive a true picture
of the world
and also perversely taking pleasure

in some of the summings-up which gloss over,
and the numbing sense of six o'clock and all's well
as though imbibing a drug which simultaneously awakens us
and puts us to sleep
sorting, cocking a skeptical ear, of hearsay into hearsay
but still too gullible, too ready to believe
in spite of ourselves

and in the end when they come on
with a bit of human interest
or a joke, or poke some harmless fun
say that's all for tonight folks
as though they would doff their bitted masks
of truth muffler, of truth garbler
and extend a hand . . .

"this evening in the suburbs of Buenos Aires
six armed and masked men abducted labor leader Arturo
    Mendoza
bursting into his home without warning . . .
the identity of the abductors was not known . . ."

Leeds

the last sunset I remember
was along a tow path in Leeds
walking in the dry yellow grass
we smoke a joint
Tony and I
pass it back and forth
along the green stream
with its old wooden locks
it flows into a waterfall falling down over brown stones
and across on the other bank
a factory lights up
and Leeds is a pale nest of fireflies
we stand in the gloom of late November chill
feeling on our fingertips
the last coal's heat of the roach
for an instant our lips glow orange
a train hurtles over the trestle above us
across the blue bubbling river
traveling the passengers to their ends
"remember Spender and his train"
we look out into the smoking twilight
and seem to see strange dwarfs
drift up from doors and chimneys
with huge heads and flushed red faces
each with a glass of bitter in his hard-husked hand
in the distance
the train sounds a faint rails echo
then darkness
lands its first silken parachutist at our feet
and the red brick of a thousand flaming houses
slowly burns to soot

lighted windows (for Judy)

Walk the night scented streets
looking always in lighted windows
hoping for a glimpse of what shines out
marking the shades of yellow
faded   homelike
the color a kind of intimate perception,
refuge for an unknown being,
shading my memories of other nights
other rooms

till coming on the remembrance of you and me
roaming the streets
one early autumn evening   after smoking

and recall the flaring promise of lighted windows
intense curiosity roused to torch-flame
for the genius—beauty
the loneliness, common fare
the complex presences
that might be seen there
the evening star risen to the second story

yet what we saw
bore so little
of what we hoped for
as though that lit-transparency
opened on a dark opaqueness
that separates us all
so profoundly
as you and I become
slowly in the rumbling
of the years
more difficult to decipher
each for each

but as I walk
in this thaw-warm night, deep into autumn
that promise flares in me again, and standing
on the railroad overpass
while a train
rumbles giganticly underneath
the worngrey city offers up its lights
and bits of lighted windows
—what's left of stars
strewn and shattered   yet nestling
in the hazy tattered leavings of the years

"out of the yellow-lit glimpses . . ."

1

out of the yellow-lit glimpses of the tables of evening
out of the concentration given to the vegetables
the dog shitting briefly in the snow before her feet freeze
the distant blare of the television which you must ignore at all
   costs
out of the night arctic in its intensity
must come the bare thread of our thoughts
just possibly wound round things

from the silencing that descends on consciousness
through sickness, fatigue, or alienation
terror, or our own madness
so forcibly implanted in us
must we rescue this resuscitant thread
and if it does not speak a river gone underground
we must follow by mute vibrations, tremoring
to where it gushes forth

2

my father would always have a workshop,
at its center fulcrum
the sinewy wornaway vice
around it the other tools arrayed in their places
with wood shavings iron-filings flecks of paint
blocks of wood or half-built instruments laid bare
in which i was never quite at home

but now i smile to think
that this small room where i pass my days
becomes my own untidy workshop
books strewn like pieces of board sawn from the main trunk
stacks of papers crammed in their holes
my old portable a vice to hold things steady
now strangely i decide if to bevel my words

to rewind the armature or balance the clock
to have my special box of screws labeled "Racconti Italiani"
or scrape down to the bare wood

in his later years
i recall my father's solitary figure there under evening lights
head cocked slightly back   peering soberly through bifocals
at some piece of work   a true and tested workman then
in the latening hours
amid the tools and constructions of his precise imagination

i perhaps less precise must struggle for some other end
but when at night i lie on my mat against the wall
the books stacked round my bed have faint sense of sawdust
and i dream that when dawn comes
out of the dark
some dawn that slowly comes and our awakening,
things begin to take on
their true proportions

Marti

waiting now as the minutes tick closer
it will fall today
love or another long spell of loneliness
it will all come upon me this evening
one of the few who really counts
will be with me or not
i look ahead to the loss of her
go on as before
getting more guts as i get older
i see the rare chance of making it with her
shining out at me
it is true life is a gamble
with odds so poor
you'd rather not if you could help it
if suddenly
you could shrug off the failures
the botched relationships
and walk straight up to it
without a faltering of courage
and smiling
with the knowledge
of the fidelity of choice
take what so rarely blooms
the trees themselves would bend to give you grace

"climbing down the embankment..."

climbing down the embankment from the bridge
river swollen to a swift pulse
under one of the abutments   balanced on a flooded platform
a fisherman, his words have quick hue
it's as though for a few seconds we know each other

walking the other tracks along the flow
thinking of those times
of long silence when nothing came
and wrestle as you might
you couldn't find the words
or rather you couldn't see
reaching you grasped nothing
things moved in you—perhaps subtlety
as though to some conclusion
but you ended in a troubled mulling
or finding words that didn't stick
—like rotten planking ripped away
moments that seemed to predominate
over the others

spring comes hard in Iowa
April—but a cold rain slants down the river
doing a short step on the ties; you see nature laid bare
the weather on a landscape in a way that doesn't lie
just what's there   old pieces of hacked off iron
rusting to their final uselessness
squat weeds by track-side creeping
starting some slight momentum of growth
like some relieving bare bones of what we are
as though I were photographer, take it in
the droplets on the surface of such a hue of dirty grey-brown
greedily the perceptions come in quick quantum moments

and remember the crew of gandy dancers

we hired on with
the ten-pound sledge flashing on the spikes
prying up the ties with crowbars
baloney sandwiches on white bread for lunch
they lived in an old pullman on a siding
some of them sweating out weeks of wine and muscatel
a few talked with broken accents
Poles and Yugoslavs with names like Masachek, Lubawitz
and thick muscled forearms that didn't come from drinking

what we salvaged from the experience
we can't quite say
yet know it's deep in our guts or brain
like a pulse or sense
a radical breakage with complacent unknowing
it lies waiting for a speechless grappling
from which a primitive value may be wrested

thinking of the old Serb
with bushy eyebrows and chiseled arms
who gandy-danced on a single rail
his worn legs moving as in a drmea from the old country
his shirt lifting in the summer breeze
fellow motleys shouting hoarse encouragement
and clapping hands as in a strip joint
his broken and generous immigrant's smile
telling us that we too, his students on the ten-pound sledge
might have our brief and flashing moments

drmea: native Serbian dance

Bartok

Bartok with his iron violin
jumping over the fields
Bartok with his singing bronze cello
his larger than life viola
playing exactly what was in your head
his Hungary that I will one day see
his music that I will one day hear,
finally dying poor in the snow of New York
Bartok with his iron quartet
enough to make old Jews weep
and tremble
in front of their hearthlike
wood radios
because he was singing the truth
and they saw it coming
Bartok's great sighing of mad currents
Bartok and the peasants out in the snow
another winter of the mind
and a clean sluicing spring
suppurating up
in a rending melodic dissonance
this screech of beauty
this agony of rich torment
these paranoid laments
that perhaps he had not even intended
and at last still the great phantom beauty
come bleeding and dancing over the rheumatoid fields

"when you live in your car"

when you live in your car
rather than a room
you get up more slowly in the morning
waiting and watching for the warm light to strike
roll out of the slightly cramped position,
and the morning blossoms
a waste field full of dandelions;
the bushes along a tiny creek will do for trees
having branches and leaves
and even the blank wall of the closed-down factory
we furtively parked behind
has its Zen-like associations
a flood of memories
something you were then
which now you can smile at, accept . . .

not having a roof, a ceiling for thoughts
and getting things going while she sleeps
you sit on the hood of the car
and your mind slowly opens to the extent of the sky
its striations, great masses of low clouds . . .
sounds and shapes seem more distinct
the singing of the highway in the distance
someone drops a tool, it clangs on the concrete
a delicate hammering with its high-pitched chink-chinking
a crow comes over the roof
with a disconsolate cry   piercing and full of curses
you scare each other when he first sees you
and flies limping off with a few choice words

you remember an evening in northern Ontario
after the long empty stretches had passed
with nothing but thick taiga on both sides
a moose that paused at the edge of the woods
then disappeared

Arctic watershed beginning just to the north
then a few fields again, farms
through French-speaking towns
where the French and Indians coexist
sometimes looking both so bleak and distraught
there was a strange monument along the road further on
you pulled off to see . . .
sculpted man woman and child
holding hands atop a stone pedestal,

"In the early morning of Aug. 4, 1963
not far from here 3 members of the Lumber and Sawmill
    Workers Union
were killed as well as 7 others wounded
in order to saveguard the rights
of organized labor everywhere."
we stood struck—
the prairie wind fingered our hair
the silence breathed very slowly
—then not at all

"This is to the memory of Joseph Fortier
born 1928, Irenee Fortier
born 1938"
and one more
brother and sister? husband and wife?
or from the same clan
and the one whose name you forgot

were they mostly French caught in some ethnic poverty
or had they, crossing lines, joined with some others—
immigrants perhaps, to struggle fraternally . . .
but the inscription in English? for us maybe
as though to say we'll tell you in the way you'll best understand

you imagine sighting down the rifles of the mounties
or the company men—the instant after they fired
into the crowd of unarmed strikers
as though from there,
seeing the cruelty of it straight on—the crimson splotches
the bloody tableau as though fixed in time
and then like a film that starts up again the cries
the fearful moaning, the agony of the bodies strewn out

the 10 pm sun cast its bright luminous Arctic glow
the black flies bit us on the neck and back of the head
they swarmed over the dogs
we walked back through the little woods
and looked at the abandoned shacks
hardly anything left—
put in a liter of oil and started off

the mornings come slowly
and more simply   if you're lucky
and other times estranged, claustrophobic, and lost
your friend still asleep in the back
you see over the fields to the lake
the mist rising slowly
something straightens in you and reaches out
does justice begin then in fragmentary glimpses
of things barely imagined?
but will of the wisp you wonder—and it's gone

for Barb

the local dogs put up a yap at dawn
as soon as they spot us
sleeping in an alley in a quiet poor neighborhood
filching some rotten wood for a fire
under the barrage of barking
I curse vociferously looking for the lost heartworm pills
we forgot to give yesterday
as mosquits hover thick as death
"this will be good practice for when we're totally penniless"
"as long as it's good for something" you say
"although I don't know what" laughing as you go
the car starts right up
like some magical animal of great loyalty
we pat it on the dash

cook our potatoes and fish in tinfoil
on the bank of the bayou
across from us a peeling orange boat "Sea Urchin"
and a grey snubnosed one "Sea Mark"
ocean going tugs?

an old drunken Franco-American stumbling in the dawn
beats a rhythm on a picket fence
sings snatches of some forgotten song

and you lie on a stone bench
arm over your eyes
as the sun comes up behind you
thinking of Easter morning in New Orleans
in the neighborhoods, with the black women
arrayed in their finery
come out for christ knows what
the great swell of mellifluous life
riffling like live flotsom
at the bayou's edge

in the wake of a boat

the bells pealing softly
carrying across the sleepy town
make the dogs perk up quizzically
some message of hope just barely perceptible to us
as we wake to the rawness doom and beauty
of a future we cannot understand or predict

things as they are

going out halfhappy
or half angry or somewhat tired
nonetheless
everything in this snow
looks back directly
with a stark clearness
as i walk through this nonessential winter's day
beautiful in a way which is neither grandiose
nor too little
all the elements have announced themselves
now they break and reform
in ways that are almost recognizable

tonight stars creak like leather harnesses
in the solitude of winter rooms
feel the harness of night around your back and belly
the icy bit in your teeth
and be pulling it alone in the dark,
know there is no way out
or through, except the long strange road ahead
in which you are the uncertain voyager
on this tramp steamer life
various companions changing through the years
like stars in patterns of constellations
burning intensely, but too far in their fixed orbits
and the special ones
that come terribly close
the tail of a comet passing over your trembling body
causing strange atmospheric disturbances
pulling out great gravitational hunks

finally always coming back to the same worn self
a cave glowing darker with experience
and less immediately comprehensible in its depths

but in summer's first fragrance
still to break off bits of the milky way
and see the evening star
rising over the blue drifting up from the sunset
and rejoice   as though you were young once more
and saw the dawn of hope rising just beyond your reach

"snow caked black"

snow caked black
greasy ice underfoot
on the low horizon the wet fog of a february thaw
curse and spit as i walk through it
suddenly its smeared beauty breaks through
the raw grey slowly pulsing in the black and white
swirling barely in the distance   quivering slightly
some joy to be granted even this
the winter's end to end terrible hack work of nature
yet man in his weak holding-out nearly indomitable
joking you think more bitter slush
another dollup of frozen grief
pile on the scalding summers
just that i live
just that you live
not so often up to it
but today laughing in the face of it
as the screw turns a hair toward spring
and what of this pain
of that wretchedness
of little matter to us
who have come so far
and who have still so far to go
who journey while falling
and who rejoice while lamenting
winter is dead long live winter

cities and years

city, dense as an overgrown thicket and absorbing its own
    humus
i push through, circulate in the veins
taste the flow of the old blood

the back door of what used to be a tavern
the same gravel leading up to something else
remembering when gino lived there
in some jerrybuilt apartment they made of it
and bert of whom it was inferred ... doing deals
certain substances now flushed away into a thousand sewers
one day gino read me a poem entitled "morphina"
about a butterfly that landed on his shoulder
and said "Gino is dead," this sadly beautiful and talking
    butterfly
this rueful spirit shaking his little butterfly head
and saying "Gino is dead"
and now bert stops me on the street to tell of the
tomatoes he grows
in the community gardens off old sand road
that skirts along the river

alleys like tunnels of fragrant darknesses
the scarred docks and refuse
as though the businesses respectable on the front streets
had dropped their drawers to reveal ...

the same tavern now rebuilt with more fake class
and the same absurd italian name
holds old friends of sorts
we smile and exchange talk
but our words will never come together again
to be more than an old and lingering affection

the river with its silences

alongside certain memories
... of the ones who have come and gone
the laughing ones because that was all they could do
to shrug it off
the tragic and grotesque ones who chose some challenge
to life, which in its hardening it could not fulfill
their darkened vision seeing the swarming under the lights
as congeries of insect instinct moth to flame

through old neighborhoods now rebuilt and strange
then pushing my way through some weeds and down a hill
i come to a barren place
the abandoned earth ripe in its desertedness,
like a small desert blooming a spring nothingness
this eloquent silence
and threading around buildings
there are walls so blank i am content and cleansed
doors shut and locked so tightly death could not enter
strangely to my satisfaction

this history retrieved that forms these dreamlike shapes
like eyes or expressions ... pensive
rooms, small green places breathing the smoke we were
emanating these faint oxides
now in the train yard they are building apartment houses
right next to the tracks, like hives
for the exploited worker bees
excavating my old buried secret senses
i say to the workman how they're building over
my old walking place, these damned apartment buildings
"yeah," he says with contempt, "they're going up everywhere"
but then smiles because it is his work "you'll have
to go further out into the country"
and under the railroad overpass, climbing the embankment
to where it levels near the top where

bridge and earth meet, where you'd sleep
if you were sleeping under the bridge,
and read the most private graffiti
in which the slurs epithets and avowals
of the new generation are penned up
"clit" "I love Doris" crossed out by "is a whore like
the rest" "we are the hate and contempt vermin"
and remember london, the east end
the profusion of youthful propaganda slogans
"China boys rule" "stamp out fascist scum" "stamp out
communist scum" "rude girls rule O.K."
"wogs out of England"
and think they must make some kind of life out of this
out of what we taught them

and the strange ones
who gave themselves to you
who lay down with you in some hidden place
the few ... you were the one for
as though you recognized each other
in some stranger dream beyond mortality
the ones ... who bestowed this generosity,
pass a cripple girl who looks at me queerly
with piteous dumb eyes and turns to look again after we've
    passed
then a shy one with small tender breasts
who says hello as though offering a small and delicate flower

in the haunted bookshop, i find a book
and read an essay on pavese before they close,
"a solitude sufficient unto itself"
"death will come and he will have your eyes"
and find an old book by carnavali
in his "last memories" he says
"oh lady death, take me, take me with you and I will

be docile as a child and I will follow obediently
in your footsteps without terror, knowing you
are the divine mistress and the divine gift to God
I will be good and kind to all those who are going the same way
I will not talk too loud and too much the way I always did in
life, I will merely stammer a few words in your ear."

cities and years sober us
an austerity mounting invisibly
like some autumn that is always coming
finally an old house where i lived, nothing but a decrepit shell
now rebuilt around the dead husk
inhabited by students who are drinking this afternoon
as though to throw off all knowledge
i show them where the old rooms used to be
now utterly transformed and the rent five times as much
and remember that downstairs was an old furnace
sometimes in the dead of winter
so much coal dust would waft up through the heat vents
the air in my rooms would gleam darkly against the lights
and you'd choose between breathing or being warm
by throwing open the windows on the january fastness
and letting the night come in

photo by Morty Sklar

Chuck Miller: A Poet Beneath Contempt

An interview, excerpted, by Ken McCullough.

Chuck Miller was born in Kenney, Illinois in 1939. He lives in Iowa in a small wood-frame house with a roomy loft, flanked by a makeshift lean-to sheltering his latrine. Miller built the house in 1984 with scavenged and donated materials, with a friend who oversaw the project. The house sits in a fenced-in grove of scrub oak, sycamore and maple, just at the edge of a cornfield. I went to visit him on a Saturday morning in early May, 1985. The cornfield was still unturned, the trees around his house just starting to bud.

The occasion for my visit was the publication of his chapbook Harvesters, *which I'd read and admired greatly. Miller greeted me at the door with his 15-year-old mutt Goober at his side. He is a rough-hewn man with a mischievous and world-weary smile and a contagious belly laugh. A friend once described his appearance as that of a Norwegian bachelor's. What follows are excerpts from our conversation.*

KEN In many of the poems in *Harvesters* you focus on the dispossessed. Your poems imply to the reader that he or she had better not live in a hermetically-sealed world in which they don't have to see any of these people; they'd better get out there and look at who the dispossessed really are and deal with them as people.

CHUCK I wrote those poems only out of a sense of urgency, but I didn't have any notion that the world of poetry was going to make anything of them, aside from those who already had an idea along those lines. I still have hopes of someday getting recognition from the larger society, but after awhile I think, well, what does it really matter. And when you get any kind of recognition at all, just from regular people who have had weird lives and have never fit in anywhere and who have somehow survived, then shit, what can you really ask for?—if you get *some* recognition, that's a lot more than a million other people get. And so in a way you start to aim for those people. In this society there are a whole bunch of people who are beneath contempt. So you see yourself as a writer who is beneath contempt, and you are writing for all those other people who are in the same boat. Well, that's just the way it is, and with a few possible exceptions, that's probably the way it will be, so why not try to see writing for them as a real possibility and one that you're going to live out.

KEN I know that the writers of the Depression have influenced your work and thought; which ones in particular?

CHUCK There were a couple who really knocked me out, namely Meridel LeSeuer, who was blacklisted for thirty years, and Jack Conroy, who wound up in Chicago writing little articles and book reviews for the rest of his life. Then there were all the others who, except for their circumstances, the times, might not have become writers. Conroy edited a magazine in the '30s called *The Anvil*. His *Anvil Anthology* has just been republished. I'll never forget this one guy in there named Boris Israel. There's a story of his, about four pages long, which is one of the most fantastic stories I've ever read. It's about a real bitter Communist who tried to come to terms with his life. In the bio notes at the back of the book it says that Boris Israel went to the South in 1936 to organize workers and Blacks, and was never heard from again. I think somebody told me he had a little magazine somewhere on the East Coast for a year or two, and he did a few things here and there—and that was it—that was the end of him. There were a lot of people like this, who make an impact on you yet there's not much of a chance to follow through on them. When I tried to locate a few of these writers I was lucky enough to find Conroy and Meridel LeSeuer still alive.

There was another guy, from West Virginia, Tom Kromer, who wrote a novel titled *Waiting For Nothing*—a fantastic book. Every once in a while it's a little crudely written, but fundamentally intense and powerful. He also had a little magazine for a year or two, and they don't know what happened to him, either. After I read that book, and while I was reading Conroy and Meridel LeSeuer, I realized that there were various demarcations within that whole schmeer of writers: Meridel LeSeuer was definitely a political writer, so she had her political cronies to connect with; Conroy was a working-class writer, so that he had the people he worked with as his audience; but this guy Kromer, he was what they called a *bindlestift*—he carried his stuff in a little sack over his shoulder and rode the rods—so that he didn't have anybody to connect with, except people hovering over a burning trash barrel, or in the soup line.

KEN Who latched on to him?

CHUCK I don't know how it worked. He did have his weird little magazine, so even he had *some* connections, but what I recognized was a spectrum shading off into people with no connections, no communications network. Kromer was a regular hillbilly. I think he went to college for a year or two and then hit the road. Many of the stories in his book are about taking nosedives in Salvation Army shelters to get something to eat and such, but the most memorable one is about some guys waiting to hop a freight, and one young kid doesn't do it right and falls under the wheels. So really, you can pick out these outstanding people who went on to become writers who are still noted but mostly forgotten, but essentially it was as if a whole generation was washed down the tubes after that was over.

The critics really trashed them out. I kept running across anthologies put together by academics. I could see that their introductions were written from the point of view of looking down one's nose at someone else—they would talk about these writers as if they were now virtually unreadable. So I thought, okay, why don't I go back and find some of these unreadable writers. Here's the name of one who fell into obscurity —Grace Lumpkin. She was from the South. I had to get her book through interlibrary loan. It was called *To Make My Bread*. A wonderful book. All the other books I had read were about hard times in other parts of the country—the Midwest, the East, California—but nothing about the South. This had an entirely different flavor. It was about hillbillies who were finally pushed off their land by a big corporation and had to be mill workers in a crummy old Southern mill town. Excellent book. I thought to myself "these are the ones that are virtually unreadable, hunh?" Unreadable to whom? To these critics, but not to me.

KEN In *Harvesters* you put a lot of emphasis on the Haves versus the Haves-not. Are there times when you look at somebody like Tolstoy, for instance, who got beyond that distinction, and think that that's something you'd like to do? Or do you think that would be unhealthy—not to acknowledge who the enemy is?

CHUCK It's a hard question. A lot of times I catch myself judging people, going out of focus with my anger and bitterness and I think that sooner or later I'm going to get beyond that or my own bitterness will eat me alive, my anger will throw me *totally* out of focus. And then every once in a while I see things in a clearer way and try to make allowances for everybody. Still, to survive you've got to be able to see who the enemy is.

KEN A few years ago I read a draft of the novel you're still working on, and could hear distinct strains of Celine. Who are the other European writers you'd consider your mentors?

CHUCK I've always liked the Europeans better than the Americans. With some exceptions, Americans are kind of provincial and academic. I've been reading the Scandinavians for fifteen years and my feeling is that they have the best literary tradition I've come across. Hardly anyone takes them seriously but they've got a tradition of intellectual integrity and honesty and writing out of their own experiences. It gives you hope.

There are a number of good Scandinavian writers, but before I say anything about them I have to say that the person who's been the most influential on me is Celine. With Celine, you've got to take into account that he's writing uniquely in French, and we're reading him in English. Over the years as more and more of him comes through the language barrier, his comments in interviews, letters, etc., give a tremendous elucidation of his theories on writing, literature, and style. In one book I ran across recently he was talking about what he was really trying to get at in his style, and that was the spoken word—the way people really speak. But he said you start with the actual spoken word, then alter it, just slightly. He said it's like a kind of underground subway that's coming along the rails, and you have to bend the rails so that it will come into the right station and make the right sound.

KEN Who are the Scandinavians you are talking about?

CHUCK There was Harry Martinson. He was a guy who ran away from home at fifteen and became a sailor. He wrote with a complete sense of naturalness. He was finally made a member of the Swedish Academy. Would Kerouac ever have been made a member of the American Academy? Never. Which leads you to believe that the Swedes have a more democratic sensibility than we. And then there's this Danish writer, Sandemose. He is the most underground writer I've come across, of the Sc Scandinavians. Their societies are a lot more tolerant than ours, but he was the one furthest in the basement, that I could find. He was just a poor guy who left home and became a sailor for a while, immigrated to Canada, then finally returned to Denmark. He hated Denmark so much that he moved to Norway and became a Norwegian citizen. One of his first books was called *En Flykting Krysser Sit Spor—A Fugitive Crosses His Tracks*. What a great title! It's about growing up in a small town in Jutland, and the enormous sense of prejudice and rottenness and horror he felt as a young proletarian kid. As a sailor and as an immigrant he got involved in some strange incidents, such as a murder and several mutinies. He's kind of an up-and-down writer, not entirely consistent; a lot of his stuff is mediocre, but all of a sudden, wham! you hit some real good passage; but he's fantastically honest and forthright—I think of him as the Henry Miller of Denmark.

KEN Do you have anything against the alchemy that's involved in making things up?

CHUCK I have complicated feelings about it, because I've tried to read American fiction of the last twenty- or thirty years and had the sense that it's mostly inauthentic, because it's too essentially made-up. Fiction, or imaginative prose, is legitimate, and yet it's got to be balanced by a sense of realism, and of one's own experience. You can see in our society that there's tremendous emphasis on making things up, as opposed to the autobiographical or realistic. Kerouac comes to mind, again—the flak the critics gave him for honestly telling what he had experienced. I remember, in one of his biographies, the biographer's quoting him as saying in a kind of total bewilderment—and I'm paraphrasing it—"Other people have been making up bullshit stories for all these years, and they're talked about as fantastic writers, and I have actually tried to tell the truth, as I experienced and saw it, and they attacked me for it." You get the feeling that somehow our culture doesn't want to confront our most crucial experiences, and it avoids them by having a literature that is make-believe. Occasionally you read a "made-up" book and what can you say—it really takes you away, but more often than not you are reading these goofy little stories, and you see the author right there concocting bullshit and you just say, what?

KEN The system of values you are working with in *Harvesters* seems to hark back to the Neolithic—a time when some scholars believe we were actually more "civilized" in the true sense, than we are now.

CHUCK The other day I was thinking about the colonists who came over in the early days of America and how they sooner or later got around to virtually exterminating the Indians, and then I thought of what's going on in Central America, and pretty much all over the world: we're still exterminating the Indian, so that we haven't really learned in four- or five hundred years, and as you've indicated, we seem to have unlearned what we knew 10,000 years ago.

KEN So you still see our present situation globally as colonists versus hunters and gatherers?

CHUCK When I was picking blueberries in Maine I saw this shadow of a resemblance to an old primitive society, and I saw how much more sense it made than our society. There was a community; not some big fantastic community where everybody was perfect and accepted everyone else, and everyone was some kind of idealized worker, but a ragtag community that existed momentarily, for two weeks. And it arose out of people camping together, working together. Then I thought about what it meant—that this was really the "lowest" kind of work, probably, in our whole system of work, and yet in some way it was the best because it allowed you to return to a primitive connection with the earth; it allowed you to connect to those other people who were in this same struggle and it also allowed you to see that these people had a certain vitality, a sense of humor, that you didn't find in too many places, as in school. We really don't have a tribe anymore, or any real kind of society. And you realize that society has really done little for you, but just squirt you out in this dead world and say okay, fuck it, maybe you'll live, maybe you'll die—I don't care.

KEN Your poem "For Joe" is one of several of yours which could easily be expanded into a novel. In this poem you bring in your own prison experience, indirectly. How central to your overall viewpoint is that experience?

CHUCK It's crucial, because I started off as a lower middle class goof-off like a lot of guys who go to college, not knowing much. I'd grown up reading writers of social protest like Steinbeck, but until you experience it, it remains somehow distant from you.

KEN How old were you when you got popped?

CHUCK Twenty-eight. I just barely survived being in prison; nonetheless, I had all these intense experiences there. It took me ten years to unscramble my mind from them. It's something that changes you unalterably, because what you see is how our society deliberately creates a massive structure of injustice in these institutions. And when you realize that people planned it out this way, it's overwhelming. You meet all these people in prison, who tell you their stories. Back then if you were thrown in for dope they automatically questioned your sanity—they sent me to the federal prison hospital division for observation.

KEN Was that S.O.P.?

CHUCK That was pretty much standard procedure. There you met a lot of strange unfortunate people who were, some of them, crazy, and still more who were trying as best they could to stay sane. You didn't know who was crazy and who was pretending and who was trying to stay sane, and you didn't know which it was best to be. I had to debate for a couple of months whether it was better to be crazy or sane, in terms of how to survive. I finally decided it was better to be sane. But it all depended on your circumstances. Some guys I knew had decided it was definitely better to be crazy, and I could see it from their points of view—they we were facing a mandatory 25 years for armed robbery; they were gambling on being crazy and had to *really* be crazy—they had to work at it.

The worst place I was, was the St. Louis City Jail. They had some real bitter violent criminals there, many of them black guys. The black-to-white ratio was almost turned around from regular society, so they treated me like Little White Sambo. And I had to watch my Ps and Qs, man, or they'd have cut me open from one end to the other. In fact, a couple of them were planning on it, and why they didn't do it, I'm not sure. This friend of mine, a couple of cells down from me, who later wound up with me in the penitentiary at Terre Haute, told me later: "Remember those guys who had the cell next to yours?—they were planning to kill you." I said "Oh, yeah?—why didn't you tell me?" He said "I thought it would make you nervous." And he was right, because the level of tension was so high there that you just barely managed to keep from freaking out. But not knowing could have got me killed.

KEN Maybe you would have provoked them into doing it?

CHUCK Right. What happened was, this one guy tried to shake me down—physically assaulted me—but I knocked him off and then he backed away, and we walked around each other like two animals. After that I guess they decided not to kill me.

KEN Did they have a reason to want to kill you?

CHUCK Here was their reason—and this gave me an insight into how crazy our society is: One of these guys was of amazingly low intelligence—one of the stupidest people I've ever met. But later I got to know him, because they sent him to Terre Haute too, and I found out he wasn't really a bad guy. He never finished the third grade, and I sensed that the environment had just totally caved in on him. So here's what he and his buddy thought: When I got my final sentence, they read it in the Post-Dispatch, but there was a mistake—it said "Teacher from University of Iowa Gets Four Years for Marijuana." I was just a student, see, but these guys read that and they said "Hey, is that you?" I said "Yeah, that's me." And they thought that it wasn't possible that anyone who was a teacher would get sent to the penitentiary.

KEN So they thought you were a plant?

CHUCK They thought I was a plant. And, after all, what's the best thing to do with an agent? Kill him. And the other guy, he was a weird funny one. He was a giant with boundless vitality and a sense of humor and intelligence. He had been a pimp. He had a voice so strong that when he'd laugh your ears would ring. Actually I had a certain fondness for him, and then I found out he was plotting to kill me.

KEN You were in for how long?

CHUCK For about nineteen months—plus three weeks in the City Jail.
  I met one guy in there whom I'll never forget, either—he was a real down-and-out hillbilly from Kentucky, a drifter who had been a dishwasher in St. Louis. He was like somebody out of Tobacco Road. I was talking to him one day and he told me about how someone had once offered him $100 to kill someone. And he was overwhelmed by the enormity of $100. He didn't have anything against the guy he was supposed to kill, and he thought it was a kind of nasty thing to do, but he realized that, in his life, to be able to earn $100 for doing a relatively simple thing like killing someone, was a lucky break for him. Somehow it didn't work out, but nonetheless, when he told me that story I felt the authenticity of his situation—that if it *had* worked out, he'd have murdered for $100. And I had thought that people didn't have an understanding of what *I'm* going through, but when I looked at that guy I thought I could just barely imagine what his life must have been like.
  You meet people like that, one after the other. There were so many American types in there—American stereopticon beings who would appear in a little kaleidoscope if you turned it just right. And I realized then that crime is the last frontier. There were all these people in the joint who would have been cowboys and muckers and sailors and explorers and trappers. Now nobody had much use for them, so they were car thieves and stick-up men and abortionists. I got the feeling that there were only two- or three percent of the population who were downright viscious, mean, diabolical, rotten. Most of the others seemed oftentimes more likeable than the everyday people you'd meet in the street: friendly, funny . . . and they knew something that you didn't, like how to be a burglar. Or you'd meet these old guys, professional criminals—real tough, with a lot of courage—more courage than I could imagine. You know, to pit themselves against the law and the massive law enforcement network, time after time; to pit their courage and intelligence, to be able to outwit the police, amazing. One old guy told me about being hung by his

thumbs in a state prison in Michigan—which was what was done then.

KEN Do you keep in touch with any of those guys?

CHUCK No. What happens is, as you leave the authorities rip you off for everything they can get. You take a bunch of addresses out, they rip them off. I took my manuscripts out, and they ripped them off too. George Starbuck had to write and ask them to please send his student his manuscripts. They sent me about 80% of them, and kept the rest. Here's the criterion I think they used: What was handwritten, they kept; what was typed, they sent back to me. Senseless, because I had typed just about all that had been handwritten. But later I picked up on the fact somewhere that there was a regulation that you can't write anything other than personal letters and writs, in a federal prison. For example, when the Birdman of Alcatraz wrote his history of the federal prison system while he was incarcerated, they confiscated it. And it has never come to light. Either they've destroyed it or they've still got it.

KEN That brings to mind something Irina Rathushinskaya said about how she was able to compose and memorize 250 of her poems in prison. She said "I used what was left of a burned matchstick and wrote on a bar of soap in my cell. I would read it and read it until it was committed to memory. Then with one washing of my hands it would be gone." Let's hope that the Birdman's history still exists, somewhere, and will surface someday.
   Have you thought about doing something with your prison experience—writing about it?

CHUCK Yeah, I thought about just writing a straightforward account of it, and still think about it. It's just a matter of having the time and having some feeling that it might eventually be published. I know that I can always crank out my poems some way or another, and peddle them myself, so in a way they are more viable than these longterm fictional things. I know I have to get back and finish the third draft of the novel I've written about my experiences in Scandinavia, though. And I've got some other ideas, like writing an account of this prison thing, and then a novel, pretty much autobiographical, in a kind of focus I know about, which is this area—southern Illinois, around the river, Iowa, Missouri, mostly about people I actually knew and what happened to them.

Ken McCullough's most recent book, *Travelling Light*, was published by Thunder's Mouth Press in 1987 and was awarded the Capricorn Book Award. His other books are *Elegy For Old Anna, Creosote,* and *The Easy Wreckage*, all from Seamark Press.